Working The Twelve Steps

Gamblers Anonymous

All rights reserved.

No part of this publication may be reproduced, distributed, or transmitted in any form or by any means, including photocopying, recording, or other electronic or mechanical methods, without the prior written permission of the copyright owner, except in the case of brief quotations embodied in critical reviews and certain other noncommercial uses permitted by copyright law. The views and opinions expressed in this book are solely those of the author and do not necessarily reflect the views or opinions of the Publisher.

© Copyright 2023 by Perigee Trade

perigeetrade@proton.me

STEP 1
We admitted we were powerless over gambling - that our lives had become unmanageable.

We at Gamblers Anonymous, believe our gambling problem is an emotional illness, progressive in name,. which no amount of human will-power can stop or control. We have facts to support this belief. We believed, at one time or another, that all of our problems could be solved with a big win. Some, pathetically, even after making a big win, found themselves in worse trouble within a short period of time. We continued to gamble. We found we had risked loss of family, friends, security and jobs. We still continued to gamble. We gambled to the point where it resulted in imprisonment, insanity or attempted suicide. We still continued to gamble and were unable to stop. We fell victim to a belief that if only our financial problems could be solved, we would be able to stop gambling or even be able to gamble like normal people. Many times we swore we would not gamble again believing we had the will-power to stop gambling. We believed a lie. We believed we had the power to stop or control our gambling. Our inability to honestly look at our gambling problem enabled us to continue to gamble. In spite of all of the evidence from our past, we still denied the turth about our gambling.

Upon entering gambling Anonymous, we must develop the ability to honestly look at our gambling. This is the first step in our process of recovery. Without honesty, we can not admit our powerlessness over gambling. We must honestly accept, admit and unconditionally surrender to this powerlessness in order to proceed with our recovery. Any reservations we had or may presently have that we can gamble means we still believe we are not powerless over gambling and that we have not admitted or accepted our powerlessness (either we have power over gambling or we don't)

To those members who have difficulty with admitting their powerlessness over gambling, they should write about their gambling, and the destruction their gambling has caused and their countless futile attempts to stop gambling. Use the "20 Questions" as a guide. Write extensively, thoroughly and specifically using each of the questions as a central focal point. Only with the awareness and the acceptance of the hopelessness, helplessness and desperation of our situation (as compulsive gambles) can we develop the open-mindedness required for Step Two.

STEP 1

We admitted we were powerless over gambling - that our lives had become unmanageable.

Step one tells us that admitting our gambling defeat is humiliating and we naturally resent this show of weakness.
1. This opposes our instincts.
2. Destruction is at hand when we gamble.
3. We are at war with ourselves when attempting to gamble denying our failure and unwilling to admit our weakness.

DISCUSS:
A. When did we first discover and/or sense the problem of our compulsive gambling?
B. Describe instances that prove we can no longer gamble normally.

In GA we discover that admitting our gambling problem to others has become the foundation on which our recovery will be built.
1. Our foundation can only be as strong as our continued belief that we are powerless.
2. Our reservations about being powerless over gambling (doubt), block our recovery.

DISCUSS:
A. Has acceptance of our "powerlessness" grown while attending meetings?
B. Have we stopped searching for answers and causes of our gambling problem and started to deal with the problem on a daily basis? Explain . . .

Step One announces we are instinctively shocked when told that will power and self-knowledge will not break our obsession to gamble.

DISCUSS:
A. How has will power failed in the face of gambling?
B. What is the meaning of the slogan "Keep it simple."
C. Have we begun to come to Gamblers Anonymous for our own personal survival — not to satisfy others?

Our failings brought us to GA. By admitting and accepting our problem we become willing to listen and remain open-minded.

DISCUSS:
A. How we learn by attending meetings regularly.
B. Are regular meetings a chore or source of relief?
C. Has our ability to listen improved steadily or are we bored at times?
D. Is Gamblers Anonymous our mirror?

STEP 2

Came to believe that a Power greater than ourselves could restore us to a normal way of thinking and living.

Having been convinced of our powerlessness over gambling and the unmanageability of our lives in Step One, we are now told that only a power greater than ourselves could restore us to a normal way of thinking and living. (THIS MEANS WE CAN'T DO IT BY OURSELVES). At this point, we must begin to develop open-mindedness. For only by beginning to be open-minded, can we start to understand the true meaning of the step. Most, if not all of our members, have found a resistance or a reluctance to deal with a higher power. The idea of a power greater than ourselves, restoring us to a normal way of thinking and living, does not come easily to us. However, if we truly believe that we are powerless over gambling and have an illness that will progressively destroy our lives, then we desperately need a solution to our illness.

In this step, we are told that there is a solution. Our solution is living a spiritual recovery program. This Spiritual Recovery Program is brought about by a progressive character change that can not be accomplished through will-power. We need a source of power that is greater than ourselves to bring about this change. The change will take place by proceeding with the work required in the remaining steps. What will come with the work is an understanding and practice of kindness, generosity, honesty and humility within ourselves and with others which will lead us eventually to a belief in a Power of our own understanding.

Here, many of us had to examine why we refused to believe in a Power greater than ourselves. We found that some of the obstacles preventing us from attempting to believe were pride, ego, fear, self-centeredness, defiance, and grandiosity. In order to recover from our illness, these obstacles must be eliminated. Here, our sponsors can be of assistance. They can share with us their experiences as to how they overcame their resistance to believe in a Higher Power. We found that writing about our resistance is a good method to help us. We had to put on paper how the obstacles blocked us and led us to refuse to accept a Higher Power.

Most of us did not fully understand what this Higher Power was. At this point, it was only necessary to accept that there was one. Many of us used our sponsor, other members or the Fellowship as this Higher Power, but eventually, as we proceeded with the work required in these steps, we came to believe this Higher Power to be a God of our own understanding. We must have the honesty to look at our illness, the open-mindedness to accept the solution being told to us and the willingness to apply this solution by proceeding on with the recovery process of these steps.

STEP 2

Came to believe that a Power greater than ourselves could restore us to a normal way of thinking and living.

Step Two warns that belief (Higher Power will remove obsession) may be difficult.
1. Many do not believe a Higher Power and/or God exists.
2. How can we proceed with our recovery?

DISCUSS:
A. Areas of success in our lives that were decided more by circumstances than our best efforts.
B. Fear of failure. Give up too easily?
C. Uncomfortable chores that proved to be beneficial.

It is recommended that all believers and non-believers "Take It Easy."
1. Keep an open mind.
2. Practice other areas of the Recovery Program.

DISCUSS:
A. Meaning of the slogan "Easy Does It."
B. Changes in our lives and behavior since we stopped gambling. Good? Bad? **Surprised?**

Step Two recommends that we stop fighting the thought that a Higher Power **may exist.**
1. Working other areas of the GA program will show results.
2. It is understood that past efforts at belief may have failed.

DISCUSS:
A. Judgments we make quickly.
B. Judgments we make on instinct (gut feeling) versus facts.
C. Arguing with others to win our point of view.
D. Catastrophes that occurred because we spoke too quickly.

Step Two promises when we have "cleaned house" our Higher Power will enter to expel our gambling obsession.
1. Open-mindedness alone is required.
2. Belief in open-mindedness is the plateau where all GA members can unite.

DISCUSS:
A. Have we started to listen more and voice our views less? When did this begin?
B. Are we open-minded or fixed in our beliefs? Why?
C. Step One of the Recovery Program.

STEP 3

Made a decision to turn our will and our lives over to the care of this Power of our own understanding.

We are powerless over gambling - our lives became completely unmanageable, then in Step Two we found that help was available. Ask yourself if you want help and you will realize that you certainly need help or you would not have come to Gamblers Anonymous. If you are going to arrest this illness, you need all the help you can get, so keep an open mind and get going on Step Three.

What must be done? At the beginning just make the *decision* so that later you can turn your will and your life over to your higher power; this willingness is the action asked for in Step Three. At this point you may protest that "I don't believe in God and therefore, this step can not be worked." It can be worked if you realize that Gamblers Anonymous is a *spiritual,* not a religious Fellowship. With an open mind start to realize that you are no longer a loner; indeed, through Gamblers Anonymous we are bound together. We are truly part of one another. This spiritual binding cannot be explained so it seems a Higher Power is at work.

When gambling ceases, a door closes on the past horrors which you have survived. A visit to the past so you won't forget to dwell there brings remorse and self pity, two deadly pitfalls for compulsive gamblers. As the door to the past life closes, the door to a new life opens. There was no faith or hope and now there is. You can see the Gamblers Anonymous program working. Then you progress to the recovery program and eventually to Step Three.

As you develop through the program things happen which seem to be coincidence, but are they? A hopeless case stops gambling, a member out of work a long time gets a job and even the ultimate happens - an insane member gets back his sanity. Coincidences? You do good things and good things happen.

Coping with each day's happiness and unhappiness is becoming slowly and surely a way of life. You must not gamble *today* and you will become better than you have ever been. Progress may be slow but you are grateful in learning what spirituality really is. Love of money is a major problem when most people come to the program. Then money falls into its proper place. It is nothing more than an aid toward a beautiful way of life; no longer is money an end unto itself. No longer are material objects the only aim and ambition. One can't buy health, humility, self-worth, self-esteem, happiness and all the other fundamentals of a serene and contented way of life. These rewards must be earned. A Higher Power and you walking side by side can work together each day so that you can become better than you have ever been. Accept this as the fruits of a master plan. Learn anonymity and other healthy parts of a sound spiritual life. By asking your Higher Power to help you get through the day without making a bet you will get the help you are seeking. That is the essence of Step Three.

How? Honesty, open-mindedness and willingness. This old formula will work for you as it has for so many others. No longer will you be lonely. No longer do you make the decisions. Life has a balance which it has lacked. In a crowd or by yourself, you are no longer alone.

STEP 3

Made a decision to turn our will and our lives over to the care of this Power of our own understanding.

Step Three asks us to complete the surrender started in Step One and decide to turn over our will to the care of a Higher Power.
1. This opens the door to the Recovery Program.
2. We will receive the full benefit of the program by more effectively working the remaining nine steps in order — avoiding a jump to Step Twelve.

DISCUSS:
A. Have we already begun this surrender by coming to GA?
B. What does our admission to being a compulsive gambler represent?

Surrender is difficult because:
1. Our independence is challenged.
2. We don't know how to surrender.

DISCUSS:
A. How we tried to prove to ourselves and others that we could gamble, excuses we made for losing, and time spent practicing gambling.
B. Pick one that best represents your independence.

DISCUSS:

Blaming	No trust	Withdrawing
Being Smug, Superior	I know myself	Material success
Judging, Moralizing	Minimizing	Dislike criticism
Analyzing	Defiance	Other _____
Debating, Arguing	Attacking, Aggression	
Justifying	Explaining	

C. Willingness is the key to surrender/trusting more? Telephoning other members? More meetings? Getting involved in GA?

Step Three promises true independence through our decision to know God's will for us.

DISCUSS:
A. How have we changed or attempted to change our behavior since GA?
   1. Have we stopped gambling?
   2. Are we liking and caring more about ourselves?
   3. Are we liking and caring more about others?
   4. Do we have a desire to grow and mature?
   5. Other?
B. Are our natural goals high enough or do we need to have "higher" goals to obtain happiness and independence?
C. What circumstances hold our interest on a continuing basis?
D. Boredom . . .

STEP 4
Made a searching and fearless moral and financial inventory of ourselves.

Trust your Higher Power and then clean house.

The first three steps have laid the groundwork for Step Four; surrender to a powerlessness to gamble and an inability to manage the problems in one's life. Then acquire a senior partner much greater than oneself to guide and accompany you through the remaining steps. Together all can accomplish so much which cannot be done alone.

Step Four - now you are into the "Cleaning House" area of your life. Now begin an intensive inner search to locate as much guilt, and good, as you can uncover. This search is healthy and practical because dormant, accumulating guilt has long been an enemy. Most compulsive gamblers covered this guilt with a clever facade called rationalization. In the past rationalization tricked us into making very bad actions seem not so bad or even good. Honesty and only honesty can break down this tricky facade. Then you can see yourself exactly as you are for perhaps the first time in your life. Face squarely the financial and emotional wrongs that have been done in order to then forgive oneself.

While doing Step Four how do you uncover all the guilt: A thorough reading of "A Guide to Fourth Step Inventory" available through your group or from the International Service Office can be of great assistance. Then, an autobiographical approach starting with your first bet or even earlier, and moving forward to the present seems indicated. As one moves along many areas of guilt long forgotten will come to mind. Perhaps you will see some of the following — over-indulgence, greed, lying, dishonesty, failure to accept responsibility, self-destruction, destruction of others, excessive waste of time, arrogance, resentment, jealousy and many others. Guilt is personal, therefore one must seek it out by oneself.

Your mind will probably turn to loved ones and the harm laid on them; The dishing out of insecurity so generously. This guilt must be fully realized so we will not be tempted to deal with it later by further gambling. In taking inventory honestly, examine each incident that you can recall from your gambling days. This includes the things you did and those you failed to do: The physical abuse and the verbal abuse which left a lifetime impression. There is much manipulation of people which took from them their right to lead their own lives.

No two gamblers are alike yet none is unique. Each of us has our own collection of guilt which must be unearthed. After discovering and digging up this guilt, one will find it necessary to rid oneself of it. The steps that follow will show how to do this. By practicing these steps you can attain a better way of life based on solid healing principles.

With the help of your Higher Power you can acknowledge guilt as you work the fourth step. Our Higher Power, as we understand Him, can do for us what we could not do for ourselves.

After completing Step Four and having accumulated your personal barrel of guilt you can get rid of it in Step Five and find that you are an O.K. person. Then the good life can be maintained one day at a time.

STEP 4

Made a searching and fearless moral and financial inventory of ourselves.

Step Four tells us that our instincts are God given, yet misdirected instincts lead to serious emotional problems.
1. The need for security, which is instinctive, drives one to become power mad and selfish.
2. Greed, lust, envy and pride are destructive habits.

DISCUSS:
A. What obsessions and excesses in our lives became a problem?
B. Are we prone to tolerate bad habits rather than change them?

Willingness to look at our misdirected instincts (defects) is pride in reverse.
1. It is a step toward humility.
2. It is a lessening of our "big shot ego."

DISCUSS:
A. Persistence to gamble after we discovered we may be destroying ourselves.
B. What experience brought us to GA/or finally started our belief in GA?

Many members feel that gambling is their only defect.
1. But we identify with other members who claim many defects.
2. We learn that a drastic change in many areas of our lives will be required to maintain the desire to stop gambling.

DISCUSS:
A. Were we prone to blame others for:
   1. Our failings?
   2. Gambling defeats/losses?
   3. Gambling?
   4. Name other reasons.
B. What does taking "others inventory" symbolize?

Step Four warns that we must be fearless when taking our moral and financial inventories.
1. Our egos have created many road blocks.
2. Taking 1st, 2nd, & 3rd inventories will give us a clear perspective of ourselves.

DISCUSS:
A. Methods for taking inventory.
   1. Written.
   2. How Often/When.
   3. Use of "A Guide to Fourth Step Inventory."
B. Pick your special defect and discuss:

Greed	Lust	Selfishness	Blaming
Anger	Envy	Rationalizing	Bad listener
Pride	Talk too much	Impatience	Other _____

STEP 5

Admitted to ourselves and to another human being the exact nature of our wrongs.

It is suggested that this step be done shortly after completing Step Four, while the facts revealed in Step Four are still fresh in one's mind. In Step Four one can dig inside oneself, as most compulsive gamblers accumulated loads of guilt. In Step Five one can dispose of this guilt and cope with every day problems. One can always look back, and must in making amends, but no longer do you have to live with your personal guilt bag.

Selecting someone to help you with the fifth step is the next chore. The person should fill two needs; one, they should have the experience and wisdom to help see the situation more clearly, and be a person who will keep the conversation completely confidential. Perhaps your sponsor will be the logical choice, your clergyman or a good friend — you must make the choice. Reread the fourth step and use your notes as an agenda. Honesty, openmindedness and sincerity will make the whole thing go more smoothly. Your ego, which won't like the idea of displaying former misdeeds to another human being, will quickly accept the healthy atmosphere. You will see yourself more clearly after Step Four and this insight will remain. Self-knowledge has no bounds. Your new found serenity will enable you to calmly listen and learn. Your awareness will really accelerate. Your relief at having disposed of this guilt will be tremendous.

Humility is a very elusive trait which seems to fly away from one who seems to feel they possess it. If this be so, you must seek to become a well-adjusted person and in so doing, gain humility which one does not realize one has. Do not take this step lightly or minimize its importance. Those who have done this step feel that guilt must be disposed of, and action through this step is the proper way to do it.

Guilt disposed of as suggested, will aid you in so many ways. Self-honesty is accelerated as you clearly see your guilt. No longer will you feel unique. Rather, you will join the human race knowing that you are not alone. What the program teaches comes true. You will realize no two gamblers are alike yet none is an original. Upon entering the program, one now feels a sense of being understood. No longer will you be alone, and knowledge of this is exhilarating. As conflicts arise, however, one tends to pull away from this beautiful union. Now, the fifth step helps resolve these conflicts and you can say to all the world: "I am a human being."

STEP 5

Admitted to ourselves and to another human being the exact nature of our wrongs.

Step Five is ego deflating and necessary.
1. We must talk about our defects to remove our guilt.
2. We must see what we were, to see what we can become.

DISCUSS:
A. Habit of lying and hiding from problems. What was the outcome?
B. Is identifying our defects (problems) 90% of the solution?
C. Evidence of our immaturity — past and present.

Many feel it is not necessary to share humiliating experiences.
1. We are prone to carry burdens alone.
2. Dramatic descriptions of our gambling behavior are only offered.

DISCUSS:
A. Has honesty with self and others improved since coming to GA? Explain.
B. Has our therapy changed direction? Tone?
C. How long can we carry resentments and angers? What happens?

Humility is born in Step Five. Our burden is lightened by admitting our defects to another human being.
1. We become forgiving by seeking forgiveness.
2. Many members feel closer to their Higher Power and man after working Step Five.

DISCUSS:
A. How peace of mind is achieved by removing guilt and/or ending a lie.
B. Describe the feeling of admitting to other GA members, at our first meeting, that we have a gambling problem.
C. To whom should we seek to make our admissions? Sponsor? Friend? Spouse? Others?

"Big Shotism" often hides our true motives or painful experiences.

DISCUSS:
A. What types of persons do we tend to respect?
B. What types of persons do we tend to avoid?
C. Who do we trust?
D. Disasters caused by wanting too much or living beyond our means.

STEP 6

Were entirely ready to have these defects of character removed.

Some of our Character Defects

Anger	False Pride	Profanity
Arrogance	Fear	Procrastination
Anxiety	Frustration	Remorse
Bigotry	Hatred	Resentment
Conceit	Impatience	Revenge
Condemnation	Inadequacy	Selfishness
of Others	Intolerance	Self-Pity
Dishonesty	Jealousy	Self-Seeking
Egotism	Laziness	Worry

Housecleaning is not easy, especially when the dirt has been building up for so long. Most compulsive gamblers slither through life hiding from themselves and now strive to remove the mask so that one can see oneself.

In Step Four, we discovered many wrongs and after this discovery, strived to bring these wrongs to the surface. In Step Five, we admitted and discussed these defects with someone else.

The relief was magnificent. For the first time in a long time, one can feel as though one is no longer playing catch up. You will feel as though you could make it if you practiced the program and asked for and accepted the help of your Higher Power.

In Step Six, these defects of character must be worked on and eliminated, if you want the best chance possible to arrest this illness. We're told that character defects and negative emotions are really disturbances to serenity. Strive for serenity and see that very little upsets you in this goal. In the old days everything was disturbing. Now, our awareness will prevent us from going back into the old way of life.

Your actual list of character defects is the best place to start. Based on your new found knowledge of yourself, select the one with which to start. One is all that you can handle at a time. If you pick your worst defect, any success will certainly help as you work on the others.

Be willing to move slowly and steadily and realize that every human being has character defects but retaining yours may lead you back to gambling. You shouldn't subject yourself to these disturbances of serenity because you will place undue burden on your recovery.

At first, you may feel comfortable with some of these defects and are fearful about parting with them. But you will, given time, see the need for change and realize that these old enemies must go.

STEP 6

Were entirely ready to have these defects of character removed.

Willingness and honesty will be required to repeatedly try Step Six on all our defects.
  1. We should become willing to mature and grow.
  2. We must approach our growth slowly. "One Day At A Time."

DISCUSS:
  A. Did our aim at maturity start before or during GA?
  B. Has our honesty improved?
  C. Are we more open-minded and willing to listen to others?

There is no spiritual effort required to want to eliminate obvious destructive excesses.
  1. Most members are prone to settle for gradual improvement and just enough recovery to get by.
  2. Many members feel stopping gambling is "enough."
  3. Any child will pull their hand off a flame.

DISCUSS:
  A. Why should our recently discovered defects be removed?
  B. Why should we attempt to "clean house?"
  C. Name defects that we cling to, and are unwilling to remove until later. Why?

Step Six tells that we have natural talents for procrastination.
  1. We dwell on our self-determined objectives and goals.

DISCUSS:
  A. Is it our responsibility to widen our limited objectives and change our personality to a more perfect character?
  B. Express your interpretation of a Higher Power's will for you. Is there a meaning or purpose to your life?
  C. Are abstaining members an example for 1st timers and newcomers?

Step Six is a pivot and turning point within the Recovery Program.
  1. Many pause and become undecided.
  2. Many balk at a view of personal perfection and the continuous effort(s) that will be required to change one's personality.

DISCUSS:
  A. What is the meaning and benefit of the slogan "One Day At A Time?"
  B. Are we the masters of our fate?..."The Boss?"
  C. Which is within our grasp: Perfection or efforts towards perfection?

STEP 7

Humbly asked God (of our understanding) to remove our shortcomings.

Now you're being asked to seek, to remove, via your Higher Power, your character defects. Is this really necessary? It certainly is! Character defects were a major portion of the reason one gambled. Therefore, keeping these defects can lead one back to gambling.

For example, let's take one defect - anger. Assume you get into an argument, handle it poorly and become blindly angry, anger turns into rage. Then you feel something must be done to relieve this terrible hateful feeling and resort to what comes naturally - gambling. In the past as you know that pain caused by anger was at least temporarily eased through gambling. Compulsive gambling is a learned, inadequate response to life. You must rid yourself of the disturbances that you have acquired through gambling.

What can be done to prevent such a relapse? First, you must have a desire to remove this defect. To realize the shortcoming can destroy you, desire comes more easily if you realize what is at stake. If you are masochistic, the desire to change may be slower in coming. Assuming you want to live, however, try to take the step as indicated and humbly ask your Higher Power to remove the defect.

Humbly ask for help? A nice guy who never hurt anyone except himself? When you've survived for so long, all by yourself, how can you humbly ask for help? Look at your track record with absolute honesty. Have you really been a winner? This honest look at your chaotic years should assure you that anger must go, if only a little at a time. You can only concentrate on one defect at a time. This is a slower process but it enables you to focus more clearly. Also, working defects singly is, for most, more comfortable.

Having selected a defect, seek help from your Higher Power. Each morning shortly after getting up, seek the will of your Higher Power daily as life's problems arise. Ask for help in reducing or removing the defect on which you will be working on that day. You must do the leg work so your Higher Power can finish the job as He sees fit.

At this point, learning to cope is a new adventure. This is something many refused or were unable to do before entering Gamblers Anonymous. It's strange at first, but each time you cope you get better at it. When you leave the world of reality and slip into irrational anger, you should now be able to recognize that something is wrong. You now have to get yourself back on the right track so you can go deal with today. Anger, the defect on which you were working still might be a problem. It will scare you when you react with so little control. Anger could lead you back to a bet via the hatred and resentment created. You're not entitled to be angry; it's an enemy, not a friend.

Each day, practice restraint until, God willing, you have formed a beautiful new habit, a positive habit. Today anger should be under control and cannot lead you back into your addiction. Feel good about that. The same procedure can then be applied to another defect. Now you can see how your Higher Power can remove defects, if your Higher Power chooses to do so.

STEP 7

Humbly asked God (of our understanding) to remove our shortcomings.

Step Seven states that acquiring greater humility is the foundation of the Twelve Steps.
1. Without this precious quality we cannot expect happiness.
2. The word "Humility" is disliked and greatly misunderstood in our world.

DISCUSS:
A. Is a humble individual a weak individual?
B. Was our gambling a show of courage and/or proof that we were different from our fellows?

Depending exclusively on our individual strength and intelligence is a blockade to faith in God.
1. Admitting our powerlessness was the 1st step to liberation from our gambling obsession.
2. Some humility was required to stop gambling and to walk through the GA doors.

DISCUSS:
A. Your growth in Gamblers Anonymous.
B. Dependence on meetings, sponsor, etc. ...
C. First meeting: Shame? Fear? Other...?

We have acquired some peace by working Steps 4, 5 and 6.
1. These humbling steps have provided a source of serenity.
2. We should face this fact and proceed to search for deeper personal objectives.

DISCUSS:
A. What is blocking our will to have certain defects removed?
B. What are the benefits of prayer and meditation?
C. Do we have a willingness to be honest, tolerant and more loving? Why?

DISCUSS:
A. What is the meaning of the Serenity Prayer? (God grant me the serenity to accept the things I cannot change, courage to change the things I can; and the wisdom to know the difference).
B. Who or what will we become if this prayer is answered?

STEP 8

Made a list of all persons we had harmed and became willing to make amends to them all.

In your fourth step inventory, you made a list of the improper actions that you did as well as the good, constructive accomplishments. In Step Six, you made a list of character defects. Now, Step Eight asks you to make yet another list. This one is to identify all those you have harmed, then, to become willing to make amends to them all.

First on the list, put yourself, — you should have no doubt whatsoever with this choice. You've harmed yourself spiritually, mentally, emotionally, physically and financially.

Have you harmed family, fellow workers, employer, church members or anyone else? What is harm anyway?

Harm seems to be abusing others and taking from them the right to lead their own lives. Family members loved us and we were unable or unwilling to return that love. Perhaps, instead, we failed to provide adequately for them. Was that stealing? Perhaps, as the addiction progressed, we stole anything we could from our family or from anyone that was available.

One thing is certain. We stole time and this can never be regained. Money problems will eventually be worked out but the time lost is gone forever. With the help of our Higher Power and the program working, one day at a time, we never again will lose time or money unless we choose to return to gambling. The choice is ours, to gamble and risk progressive deterioration or not to gamble and develop a better way of life.

Did we lie? To whom and how much did we lie?

Good judgment in making this list is vital. Do not assume harm. Look at each instance and list it if you feel you did harm to another. A good yardstick is to ask yourself whether omitting a name might later return to "bug" you. If yes, add that name. Let's say you wasted many hours at work as you waited and prepared your gambling actions. Now, in your new way of life, you can show your boss someone with a clear mind who can work properly giving more than is expected.

If goods or monies were stolen, all should be returned in a practical manner. A second story man can hardly return his ill-gotten gains without endangering himself and his family; but, he might leave money in an unmarked envelope to atone for the theft. So, these harms should be listed. The method of making restitution will be determined in the step which follows. To be forgiven, one must first forgive others and then one's self. Therefore, don't leave off the list a person harmed but who had also harmed you. The entire aim is to set right the harm one has done — nothing else matters. This step is starting your return to society. Properly done, all fear will dissipate and you will be free to talk and move about as a normal person.

The list should include **everyone** you have harmed. After having the willingness to make amends, you will be able to resume a beneficial role in society, usually for the first time in many years.

STEP 8

Made a list of all persons we had harmed and became willing to make amends to them all.

Step Eight is the beginning of our public relations policy and the end of isolation from our fellows.
1. A fascinating adventure with our new found knowledge.
2. Back-tracking to survey human wreckage is required.

DISCUSS:
A. How we harmed others by gambling?
B. Injuries that we caused to others are festering. What are we doing about them?

Our first obstacle in Step Eight is our defensive attitude.
1. We focus on wrongs done to us.
2. Step Five was tough enough...let's observe some of the good we have done.

DISCUSS:
A. Blaming.
B. Do we dwell on our limited successes? Do we avoid painful views in the mirror?
C. Enemies who became friends. Why?

Step Eight asks us to make a "deep and honest" search of our true motives and actions.
1. We may feel we mainly injured ourselves.
2. Why list people who may not know they were injured and harmed?

DISCUSS:
A. Our anger and impatience. How these affect and tax others.
B. Specific harm done to others ... not monetary.
C. Should our "list" enlarge as we recover from gambling?
D. Are we manipulating and pressuring any loved ones today?

We are advised to use a "quiet" objective view to identify harm done to others.
1. Avoid extreme judgments and exaggerations.
2. Avoid building unwarranted pressures.

DISCUSS:
A. Meaning of the slogan "Don't try to solve all your problems at once."
B. Is self confidence growing in GA ... or are we getting "cured?"
C. Meaning of the slogan "Easy Does It."

STEP 9
Made direct amends to such people wherever possible, except when to do so would injure them or others.

To make direct amends means making amends in person whenever possible. If miles apart makes such a meeting impossible, a phone call, perhaps, followed by a letter, would fit the bill. In regard to the method you choose, the question one must ask is: Am I following the program and taking my lumps or seeking a softer, easier way? One must be satisfied in one's own heart that you did the harm and likewise you must be satisfied with the method chosen to make amends.

Which amend should be made first? Look back to Step Four and it's quite possible that you have already made or started to make amends. Sometimes pressure makes this decision, although that may not be the best way. Loan sharks might scare you more than bookies so you may react to fear and start with them, bookies may come next, then banks. Last may come friends and relatives because you don't fear them; in truth, they should probably be first on your list except for a crime you've committed which may lead to court action and incarceration.

The solution to these questions may be found in an effective pressure relief group meeting. Usually amidst all the confusion, it will be suggested that each creditor be asked for a moratorium. This extra time will permit a chance for a pressure relief group meeting to be held and a course charted which will, in time, rid one of all the pressure of debts and bring manageability into the new way of life.

This pressure relief meeting can cover marital, legal and financial areas.

It is an objective approach — help will come from experienced people who once were in the same shoes. The success of such a get-together depends on complete openness, spouse's willingness to cooperate in the plan and continuing desire to follow the plan to the letter until completed. It is equally important that the single member also have a pressure relief group meeting. As one approaches those harmed, one may assume to know how they will react to the effort. Try not to predict their reactions — their reaction is not predictable. At this point honesty is neeeded.

As long as this honesty is present, you can correctly present the harm and how you intend to try to make amends for this harm. One may be facing a long period of paying back debts; in some rare cases, perhaps, the task will take a lifetime. Remember, it took a long time gambling to get to this point and it may take a longer time to repay. Recovery from addiction is a lifetime process. These wrongs can be corrected by practicing the Steps in your daily life. One may hear in Gamblers Anonymous, "You must walk the way you talk." As one practices the Steps, personal growth will result and family will benefit. Abstaining from gambling, working the program and making amends, you will gradually return to society. Self-respect, so long absent, starts to return.

Making amends does not always mean just repaying. You may not have taken money from your in-laws. You might have treated them very poorly or with indifference — Also think about your fellow workers, teachers, neighbors, etc.

STEP 9
Made direct amends to such people wherever possible, except when to do so would injure them or others.

Good judgment will be required to take Step Nine.
1. Timing and prudence are needed.
2. We will also need courage.

DISCUSS:
A. Has anger diminished? Can we deal with problems clearly and objectively?
B. Today, what personal consequences are unacceptable? What fears remain?

Having made a list of those we harmed ... we saw that "groups" of individuals are divided.
1. Some will be seen now, later or never.
2. Some opportunities to make amends have been passed.

DISCUSS:
A. Procrastination. Too much thinking and not enough work with personal problem solving and growth.
B. Reasons for not making amends when opportunity arose. What to do at this point?

Step Nine warns we can only freely admit damage and apologize when . . .
1. We are reasonably certain we are recovering in the GA Program.
2. We are sincere.

DISCUSS:
A. Current growth in GA.
B. Need for "self honesty." Has awareness of "self" improved?
C. Have self esteem and confidence grown? Explain ...

Making amends may jeopardize our employment, family relations and personal friendships.
1. Frankness is the best method.
2. When in doubt, seek help from Higher Power, GA group or sponsor; seek guidance.

DISCUSS:
A. Difference between fear of consequences and shame of apologizing.
B. Meaning of "Serenity Prayer."

STEP 10

Continued to take personal inventory and when we were wrong, promptly admitted it.

Now that we have progressed through the first nine steps we should be ready to maintain them with the last three steps. Each day, take an inventory. This inventory is for today only and it shows quite clearly if the day has been used wisely or not. The daily balance sheet will help you see personal growth as you realize that you are accomplishing things which you could not do before. This is a good feeling which gradually increases self-worth and self-esteem. Changing "Love of self", a fantasy, to "Self-love", is a reality.

In taking an inventory, look for personal growth, not perfection. For example, make a list containing five items you want to achieve. At night the inventory might reveal that you accomplished three. Be happy with three. Remember the many days, months and even years, when you tried to think of even one thing of a positive nature that you had done. Seek daily progress, not perfection. Growth may be slow and small but be grateful for progress. The ability to cope is perhaps the most valuable reward which you will receive from the program. One no longer has to avoid a problem by ignoring or side stepping the issue. With some problems, particularly at first, you may cope weakly. So what? Don't avoid responsibility, and as you cope on a daily basis you will become more skillful. One day at a time becomes a life time. Some of us tend to be over achievers; we tend to take on tasks for which we are not yet ready. Either we are too new in the program to handle such a problem or we are too ambitious. Take it easy, a little progress each day is a great reward. Perhaps two questions we might ask ourselves each day are these — Did I help another person today? Did I contribute to harmony in my world today? It is suggested that no major changes be made during the first two years of abstinence. The mental and emotional imbalance we brought to Gamblers Anonymous needs time to heal. After two years our thoughts are much clearer and success much more reachable. Abstinence combined with physical, mental and emotional healing will give us a logical ability to cope.

The second part of the step is sometimes more difficult. To promptly admit to being wrong means that one has become a little humble and that can rid oneself of deceit, arrogance, false pride and other character defects. If you can admit to being wrong right now, you are truly gaining a deeper insight into yourself. Freely admit the other party is right and being glad for them, even appreciating confrontation and constructive criticism is a giant step. This step and the two which follow if done each day will help maintain daily growth. Another view is that Steps One through Nine are never done and should be regularly repeated.

STEP 10

Continued to take personal inventory and when we were wrong, promptly admitted it.

Step Ten tells us to put our GA way of living to practical use.
1. To maintain the desire to stop gambling.
2. To maintain emotional balance under all circumstances.

DISCUSS:
A. How can we carry our GA way of living into our daily lives?
B. What particular circumstances "tick" us off and create anger?

We cannot make much of our lives until we form the habit of self appraisal (taking regular inventory).
1. Our first objective is to restrain angers, actions and judgments which encourage impatience.
2. Create insurance against our return to "big shotism."

DISCUSS:
A. Do we "think" before we speak? Are we prone to snap judgments?
B. Are we less angry since coming to GA? Why?
C. Are we still slaves to our emotions?

Daily inventories will become routine, not the unusual.
1. Calming the moment.
2. Deciding who is right and wrong.
3. Revealing our true motives.

DISCUSS:
A. Do we still justify our feelings of anger?
B. Tolerance of others. Has it improved? Why?
C. Is saying "I'm sorry" painful?
D. If apology is becoming easier ... when did this start? Why?

Delay of apologies and procrastination is a defense.
DISCUSS:
A. Why should we promptly admit wrongs?
B. Having a "defense" signifies a war or contest. Who are we fighting? Why?
C. Hiding...

STEP 11
Sought through prayer and meditation to improve our conscious contact with God as we understood Him, praying only for the knowledge of His will for us and the power to carry that out.

It should feel good to be into the maintenance steps. Step Eleven asks us to improve our conscious contact with God as we understand Him. Steps Two and Three made us aware that human resources were not enough even though when most entered Gamblers Anonymous they felt such human help would be sufficient. Eventually we came to realize that our addiction meant we must use all possible help. Now we must learn better how to communicate with our Higher Power. How can we get the most help available? How can we combine Higher Power help with human help? We will need both.

Back in the gambling days such communication was virtually impossible. Then most felt unworthy, ashamed and cut off from this visual contact. We sought help but offered nothing of ourselves. When one feels cut off, one doesn't make any effort to communicate with one's Higher Power.

As one approaches Step Eleven two points seem important. One, is whether this step helps control ego? Does one need the step? Talking with other members, you will be told that you need all the help that you can get. Also you will be told that some problems which may be your lot cannot be solved by human resources alone. The help is available so decide to use it. Whatever it takes, do it to avoid a return to gambling or the personality of the compulsive gambler.

The second point to be considered is ego. Those that have been in the program a while see how capable of change ego is. For extreme unworthiness, ego can expand to a very large unhealthy size in seconds. When ego swells the mind closes to new ideas, particularly those that are not one's own. Then one's Higher Power becomes unnecessary. "We can do it ourselves".

It's time we scrapped this way of thinking and replaced it with one which accepts a Higher Power as the boss and which, therefore, will not swell to an unworkable size. As you grow in the Gamblers Anonymous Program, ego will become more healthy as you learn. Old ego, the source of much stress, discomfort, impatience and anxiety will be replaced by a peace loving serene ego.

A conscious contact seems to start with daily prayer. What is prayer? To some it is a personal chat with their Higher Power. So each of us can pray as we see fit. Realizing your weakness you will seek the will of your Higher Power and the strength to carry it out. Seek your Higher Power's will as you are blind to the master plan. Daily, thank your Higher Power for mercy in showing you His will.

At first prayer is difficult and you can "fake it until you make it". In time you will grow to eagerly accept prayer and know the rewards it will give you. As you try to cope with the new problems life offers each day, prayer enlarges the ability to cope.

Meditation is prayer at an even deeper stage of spiritual development. If one prays the serenity prayer, effort at concentration is on the entire prayer. If you were to meditate you would concentrate on one word or one small group of words. Serenity, courage or wisdom would be a good place to start. A word examination like this makes the prayer more meaningful and makes you more aware of your place in the human order. This is a bare beginning in meditation and will help you to develop this meaningful practice.

The bottom line seems to be a more complete recognition of yourself in relation to God and human beings. Your success is now His and your failures, accept as your own. Seek to learn from the failure.

God will give you the strength to carry out His will if you seek His will and His strength.

STEP 11

Sought through prayer and meditation to improve our conscious contact with God as we understood Him, praying only for the knowledge of His will for us and the power to carry that out.

Step Eleven outlines the promise that prayer and meditation are the means to conscious contact with our Higher Power, but ...
1. Some members feel that this contact is unnecessary.
2. Many cling to "G.A. is my Higher Power" and contact is always available.

DISCUSS:
A. Miracles of recovery witnessed in G.A.
B. Is recovery accomplished alone or with the help of others? How have others in the program contributed to our personal recovery?

Those who experiment with prayer and meditation find unexpected results.
1. Closed-minded members will not try.
2. Prayers to resolve specific problems are a demand to have God conform to our will. Continued exploration of prayer and meditation is suggested.

DISCUSS:
A. How has open-mindedness and concern for others improved?
B. Have we become interested in improving our spiritual values?
C. Can we become the "old dog" learning new tricks?

Examination of any prayer will be helpful.
1. Read slowly.
2. Self forgetting is the goal of all prayer.
3. Debate and comments do not apply to experimentation and efforts at prayer. Here ... we are on our own!

DISCUSS:
A. "It is better to give than to receive." Why?
B. When did you receive your last compliment? About what? Was it deserved?

Imagination is the food of sound achievement. Meditation and prayer are the food of our soul's growth.
1. We find spiritual objectives through prayer.
2. A conscious contact with God to know His will for us offers true freedom.

DISCUSS:
A. Our new values of truth and honesty - are they paying off?
B. Our greatest source of personal satisfaction these days. Peace of mind? Freedom? How did it happen? When? Why?

STEP 12
Having made an effort to practice these principles in all our affairs, we tried to carry this message to other compulsive gamblers.

This is the most popular step of all; even brand new members want to give of themselves. The bottom line, however, seems to be that one cannot give away something that one does not have. Saying it another way, you cannot carry the recovery program to another unless you are practicing the twelve steps in your life, one day at a time. Then you will have a strong message to carry.

Ask yourself if this is a spiritual program and it is. The chances are that your spiritual bankruptcy was complete. Most of us early in our gambling career abandoned our spiritual values. Now as these values are returning and with gratitude you will want to share them with other members as once they were shared with you. Listening and hearing what the other members are experiencing is probably the first opportunity you will have to help. Sometimes we teach when we should be listening. Listening itself will communicate to others your personal understanding of what they are saying. Let's reflect. Do you remember how low in self-esteem you were when you attended your first Gamblers Anonymous meeting? You had no faith and therefore no hope. As you listened and talked and eventually looked at yourself and the others (who seemed happy around the table) faith and hope slowly returned.

Recall that the first member you met came to the meeting early, arranged the table, put out the combo books and put on water for coffee. Was he working Step Twelve? Yes, by showing you he cared for you and all the other members. Caring seems a prime and necessary ingredient in order to work this Step. If you don't care, how can you share?

Then this caring member told you that the program was and must be self-help. Then, he explained another Gamblers Anonymous paradox. If you give of yourself and try to help another human being, you will gain from the act of giving even if your effort fails. It is in giving that we receive and so it becomes self-help. Remember two words — effort and tried. Success in this Step is putting forth the effort and trying to carry the message — not how many heard you or followed your advice.

When you left the meeting you had to return to the wreckage you had created. You gave your phone number and received a phone list. You were probably too shy and ashamed to make a call but within the next day or so a member called you. It wasn't so much what was said as the fact that someone cared enough to call. This serves to revitalize your faith and hope. Again, caring embodies all the nice elements of spiritual growth.

As you started to come out of the fog; you had a sponsor and hoped he would give you the time, experience and wisdom. This unwritten contract to help another seems the highest degree of working Step Twelve; it is caring at the highest level.

Following are some of the many ways by which one can practice Step Twelve:
Be an example of quality abstinence.
Accompany another member on a Twelve Step call.
Visit sick members.
Phone members.
Chat after meetings with new members or those with problems.
Assume some of the duties, obligations and responsibilities of the Fellowship.
Explain your disease and how you arrested it to relatives, doctors and employers.
Tell your story to help a fellow member.
Do public relations work.
Practice the Gamblers Anonymous Program.

STEP 12

Having made an effort to practice these principles in all our affairs, we tried to carry this message to other compulsive gamblers.

Step Twelve offers us the opportunity to use our new knowledge and GA experience. Putting it to work! Success means trying.
1. Helping other compulsive gamblers in and outside the fellowship.
2. "Giving" which demands nothing in return.

DISCUSS:
A. Are we ready and willing to help others?
B. What does "ready" mean and can we help others as "newcomers?"
C. What is 12 Step Work? Sponsoring, telephone calls, clean-up, etc. ...

We find in Step Twelve that we have received a special gift by working the entire recovery program.
1. Life is not a dead end. There is purpose to life.
2. We are now an example of "recovery" through the GA Program.

DISCUSS:
A. Personal experience with previous 11 Steps.
B. Is the job finished?
C. Why do many members say "I am a grateful compulsive gambler?"

Some members are prone to "two stepping" - working only Steps One and Twelve.
1. Sponsoring other members becomes discouraging.
2. We often give advice where we are not qualified and then feel hurt when we are rejected.

DISCUSS:
A. Guiding new members — GA suggestions.
B. Do we tend to over-manage circumstances? Can we be too involved in a member's recovery?
C. The need to attempt to work all twelve steps.

We can carry our GA spirit into our daily affairs.
1. Adjusting to all conditions.
2. Our GA efforts provide the tools to overcome wearying problems which plague the unprepared.

DISCUSS:
A. How we reflect and see our growth in the angry and confused behavior of others while we are calm and confident.
B. What your personal ABSTENTION from gambling symbolizes.

www.ingramcontent.com/pod-product-compliance
Lightning Source LLC
LaVergne TN
LVHW040204080526
838202LV00042B/3319